Simone Kaplan Special Edition :Black & White

Photograpy Book (Special Edition)

Black & White

Dedicated for W.K.

Copyright©2013 by Simone Kaplan

Coverpicture ©13 by Simone Kaplan.

All Rights reserved by Simone Kaplan

Mysterious Wood

The wood has a little bit mysterious in itself.
The sun sent her rays by the countless branches and thereby conjured up a mystic mood. So long the sun seemed, I was happy and worked keenly with the camera around this mood to catch.
However, when the sun slowly disappeared behind the trees and the shades became disastrous longer, I caught my camera and whizzed by the wood in the saving free field.:)
Who knows what is hidden there thus everything behind the black, dark, mysterious trunks and you secretly observed.... brrr

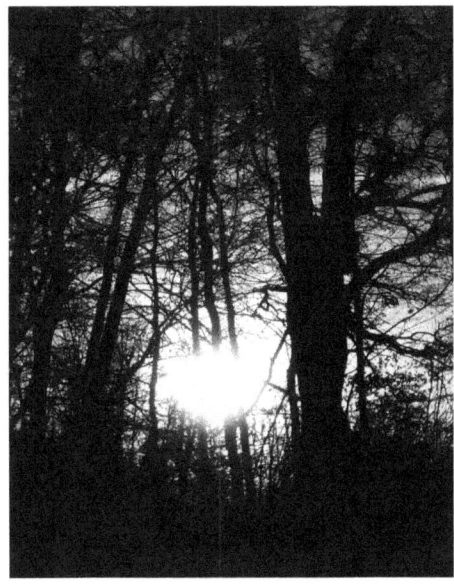

Simone Kaplan　　　　　　　　　　　　　　　　　　Special Edition :Black & White

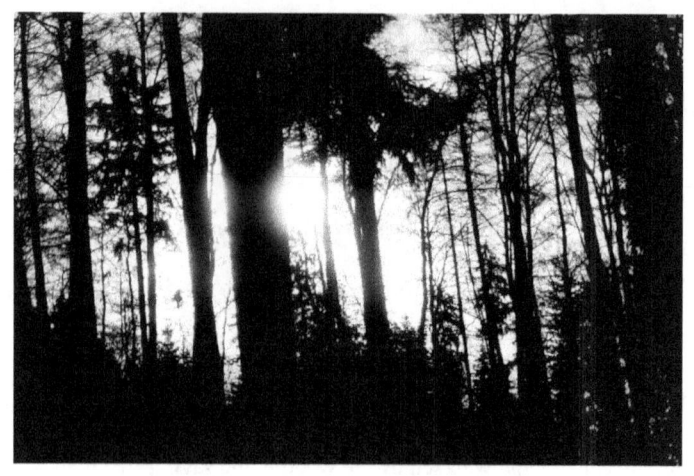

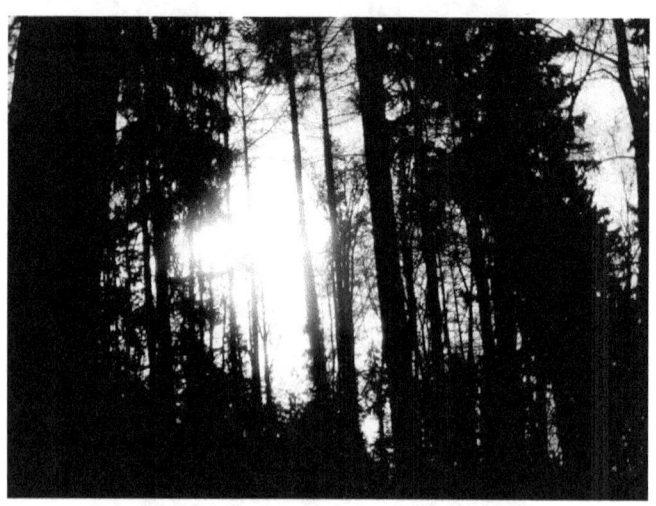

Simone Kaplan   Special Edition :Black & White

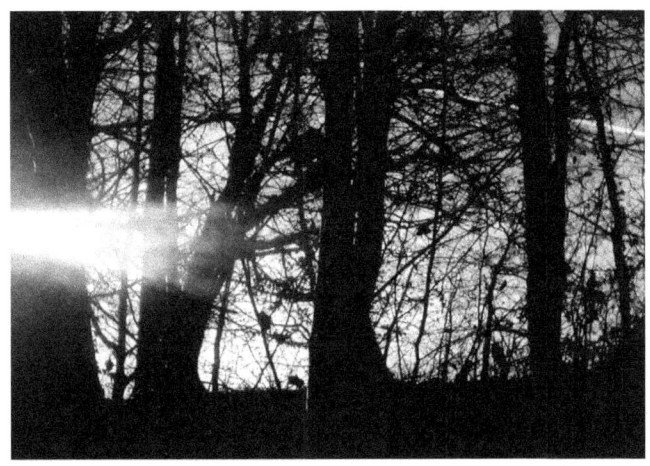

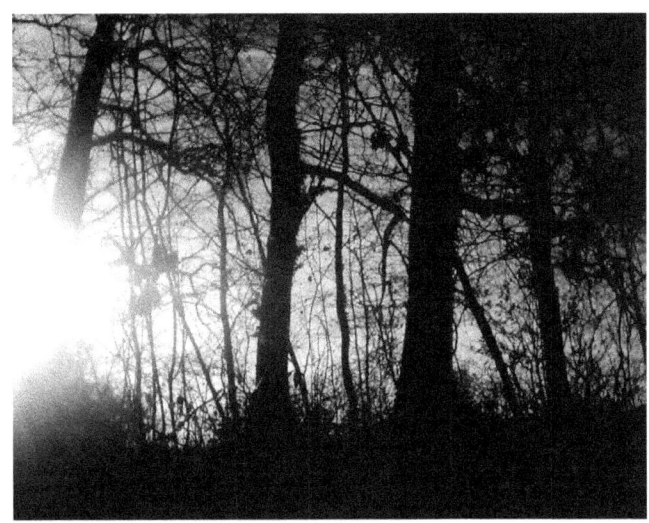

Simone Kaplan Special Edition :Black & White

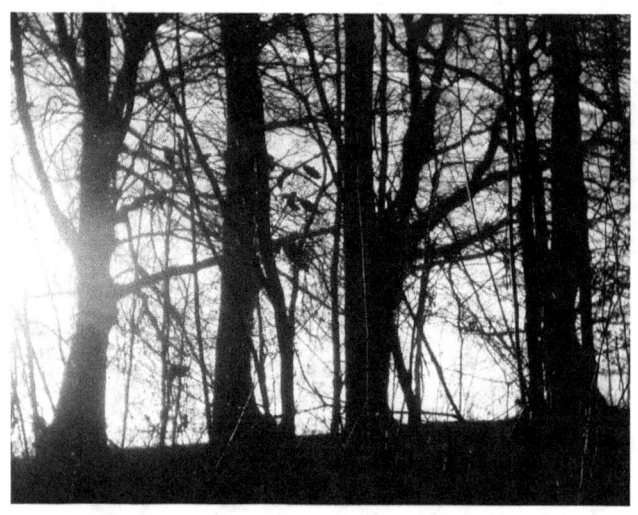

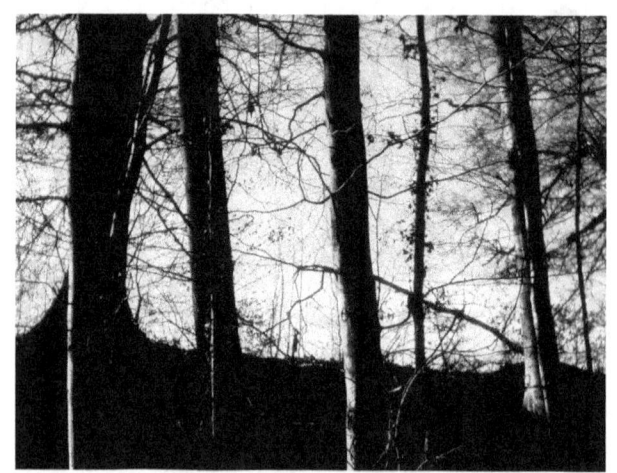

Simone Kaplan   Special Edition :Black & White

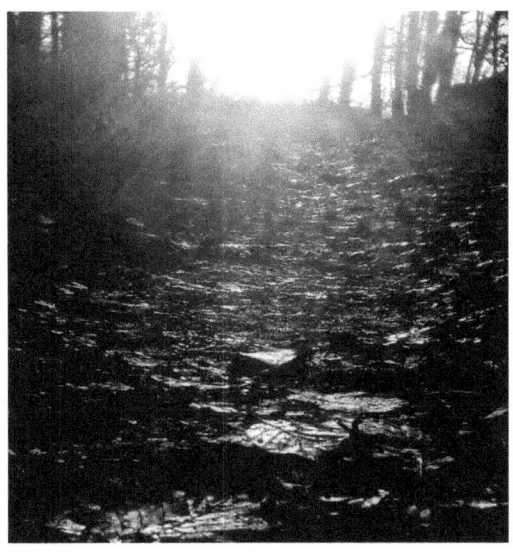

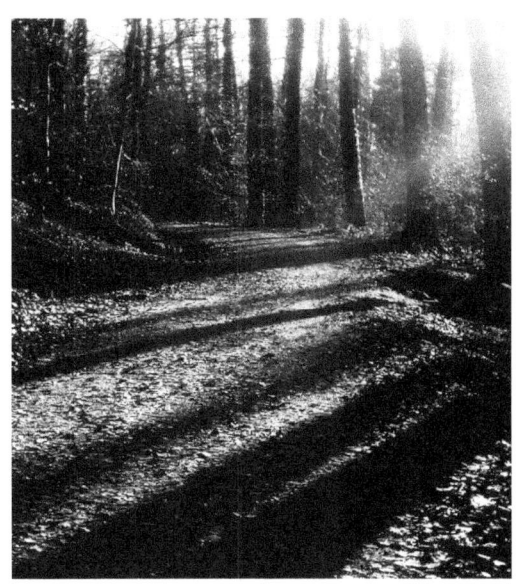

Simone Kaplan   Special Edition :Black & White

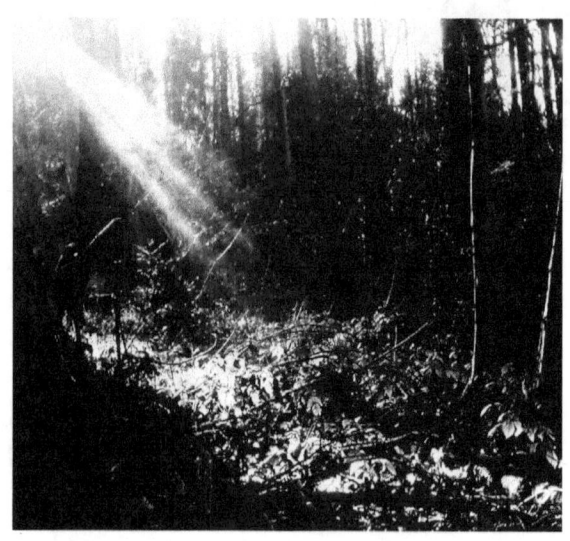

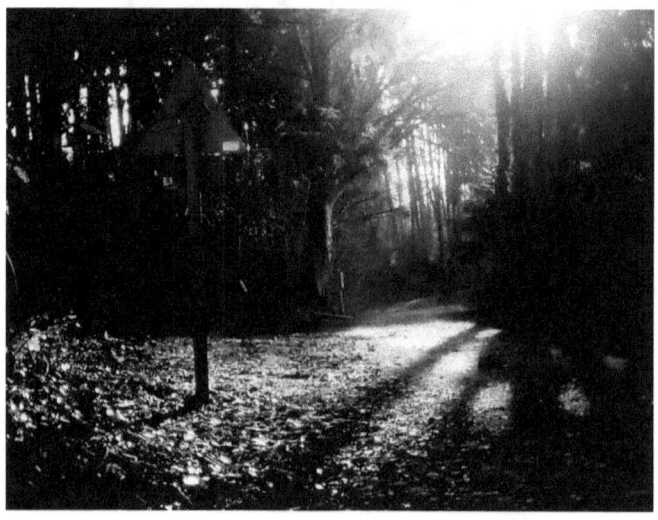

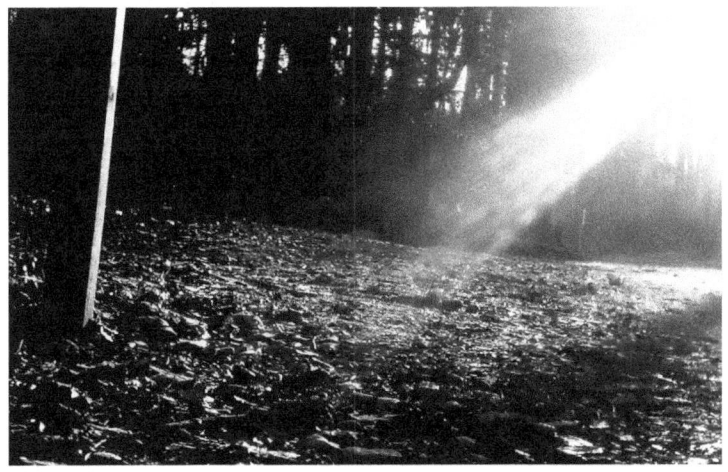

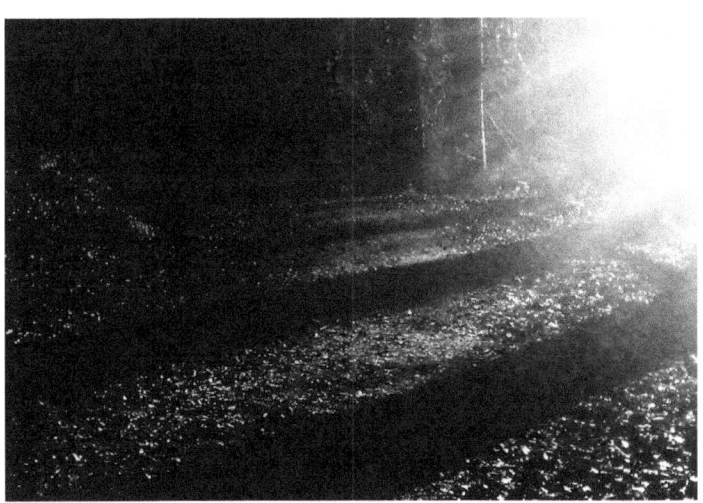

Who knows..... what himself behind the menacing darkness hides.... Horror purely.

Simone Kaplan   Special Edition :Black & White

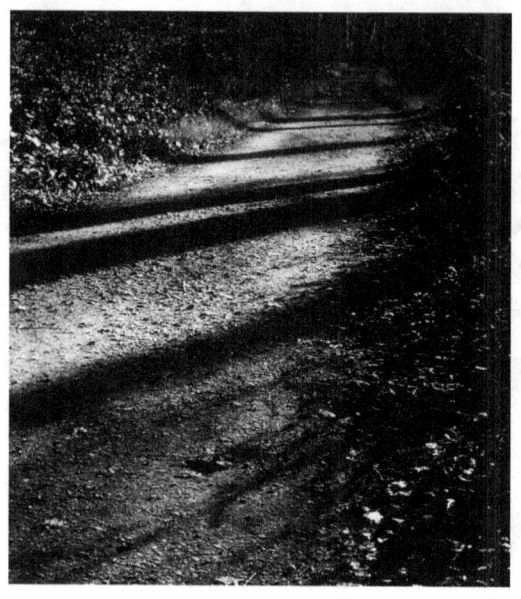

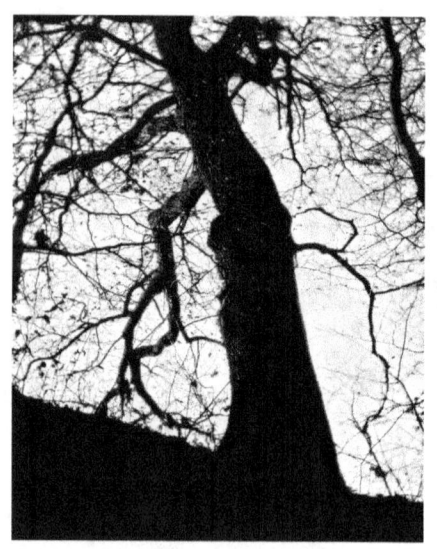

Streetmoments

Streetmoments means, to catch the moment on the street . One of the most difficult subjects in the photograph. Since the pedestrians should feel very unobserved. Now... quite difficultly if I stand there before them and hold to them a camera in the face ….:)
So I had considered a trick.
I acted in such a way as if I took a photo of a building. However, in secret I had the pedestrians in the picture.Therefore I moved like a big cat who was on deerstalking. The pedestrians noted nothing of my true intentions and ran directly in my camera. I snapped directly. Besides, out there came these pictures .:)

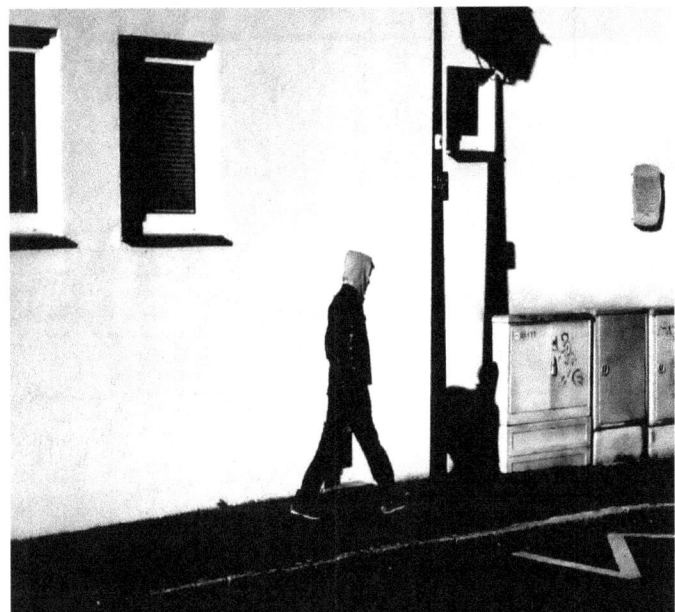

Simone Kaplan　　　　　　　　　　　　　　　　　Special Edition :Black & White

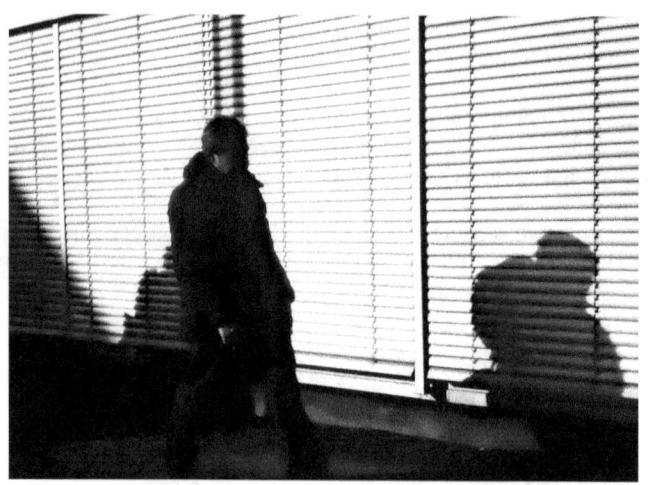

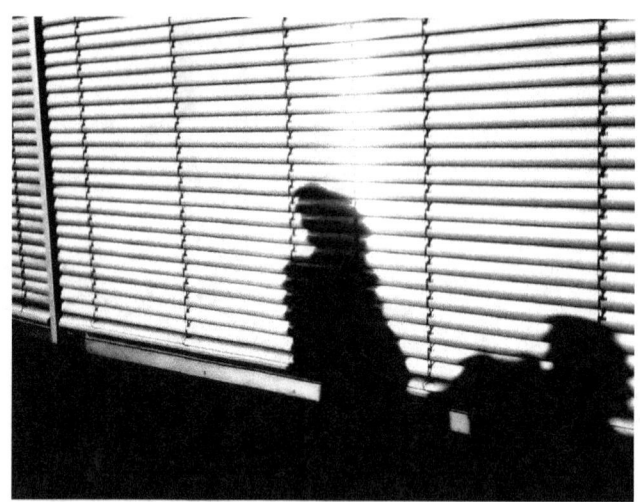

Simone Kaplan   Special Edition :Black & White

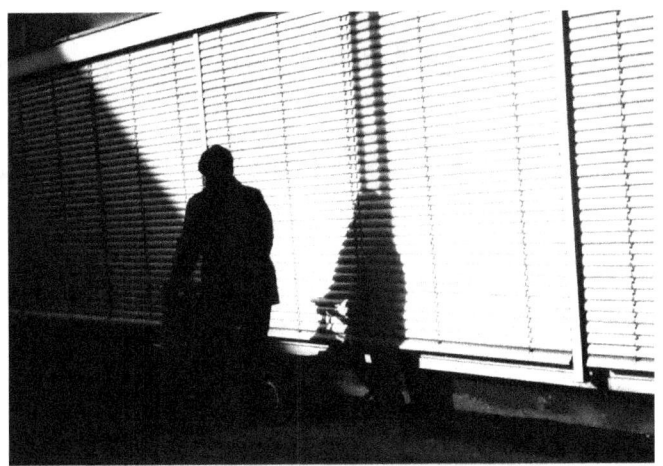

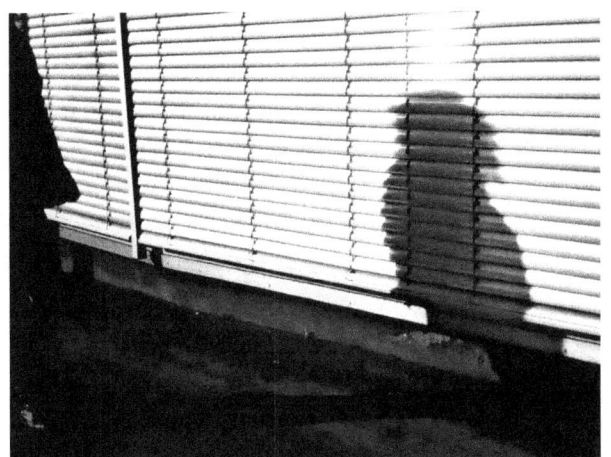

Simone Kaplan Special Edition :Black & White

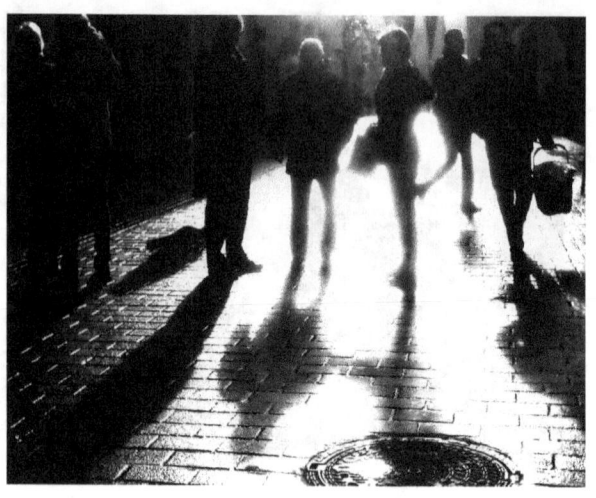

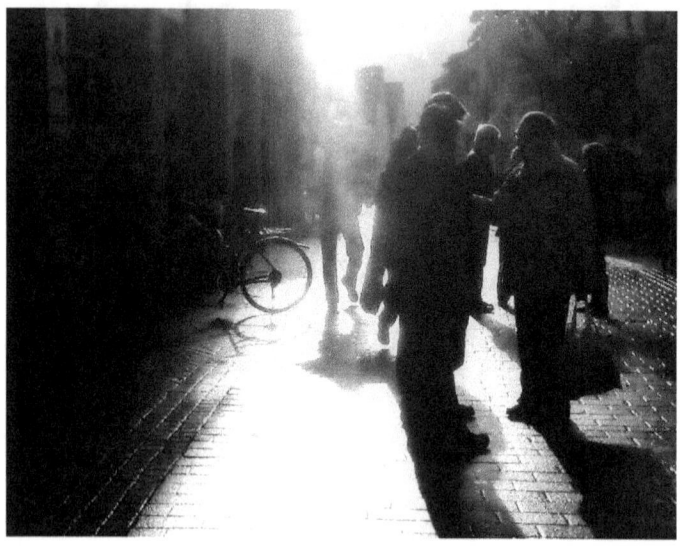

Simone Kaplan   Special Edition :Black & White

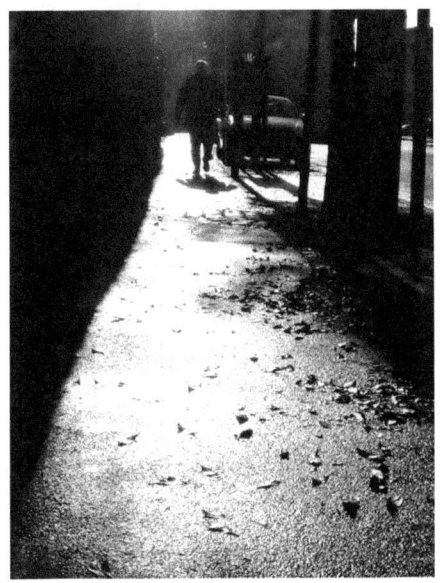

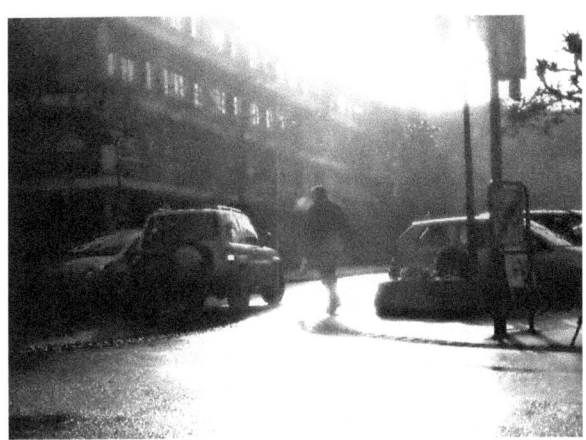

Simone Kaplan   Special Edition :Black & White

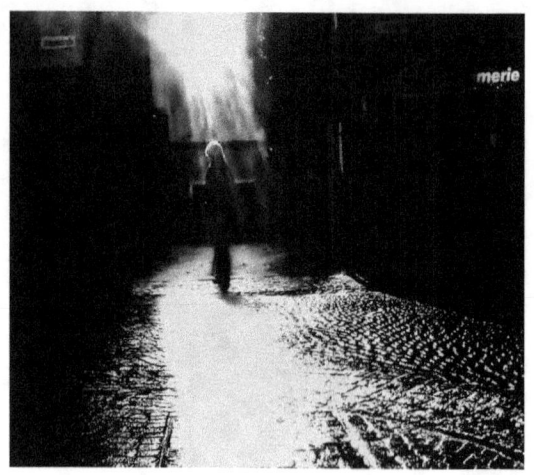

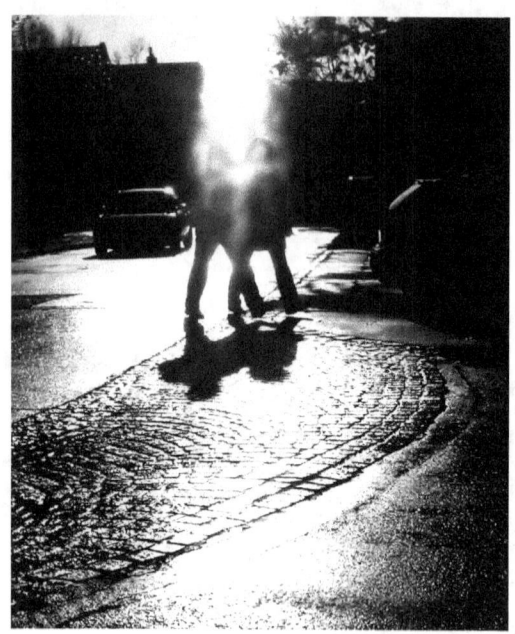

Simone Kaplan   Special Edition :Black & White

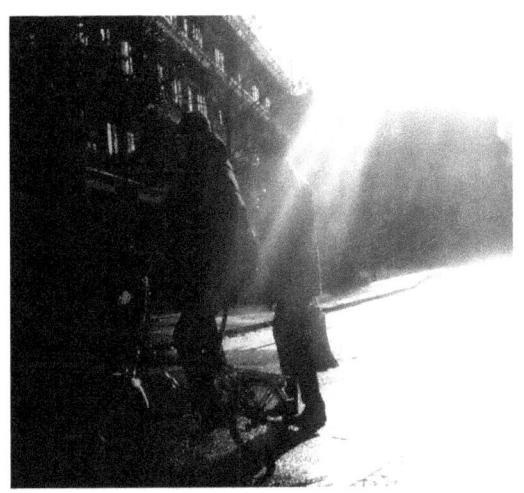

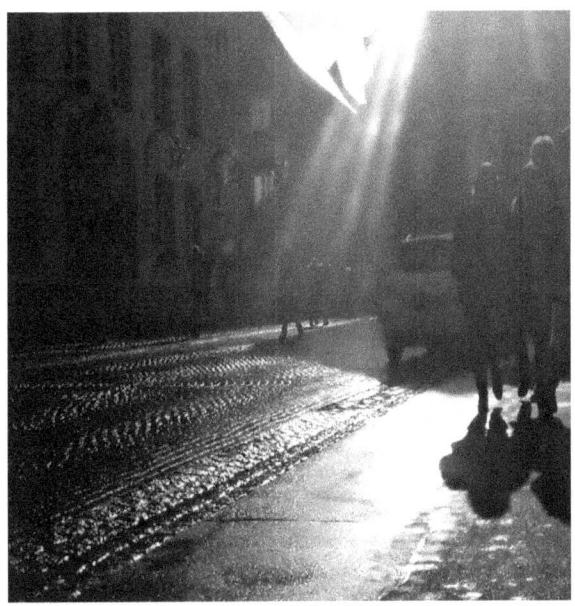

Simone Kaplan Special Edition :Black & White

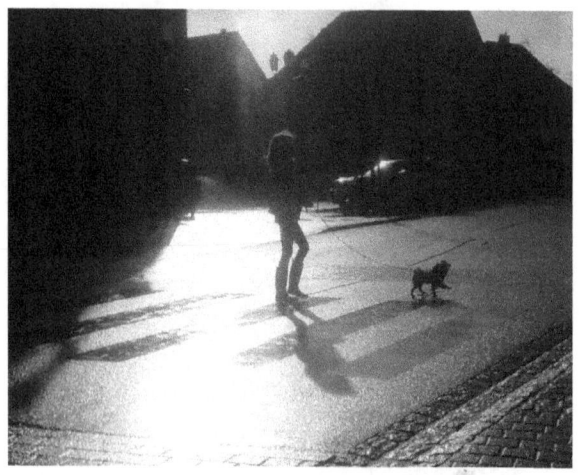

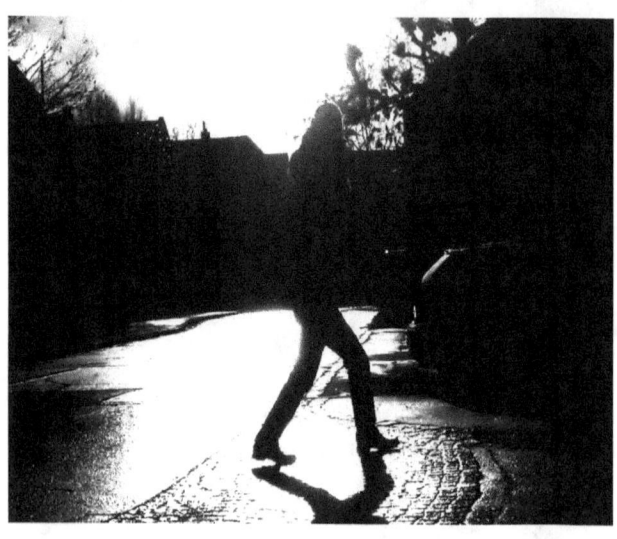

Simone Kaplan　　　　　　　　　　　　　　　　　　　Special Edition :Black & White

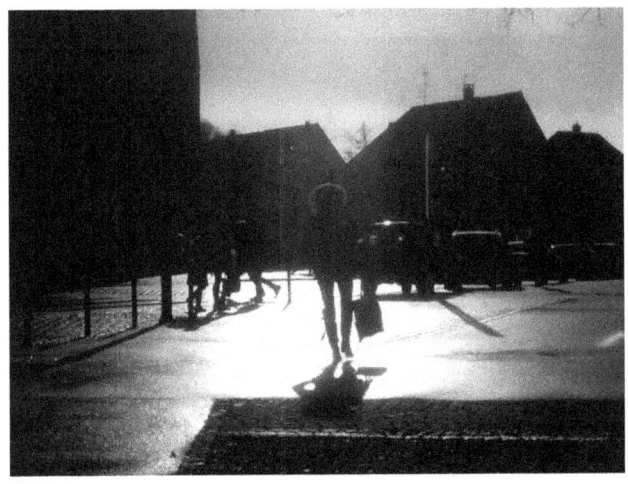

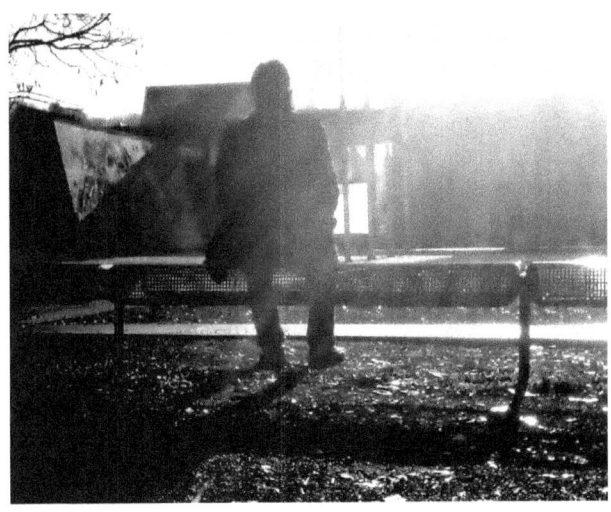

Simone Kaplan   Special Edition :Black & White

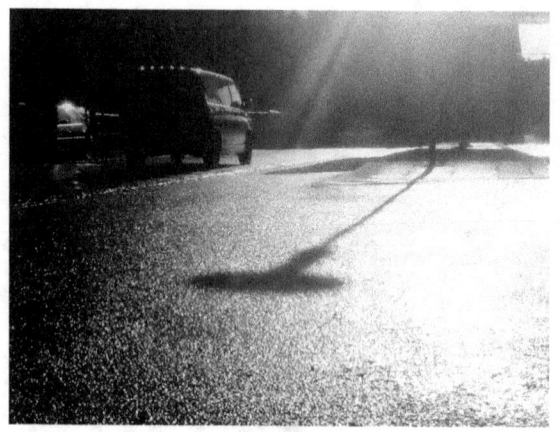

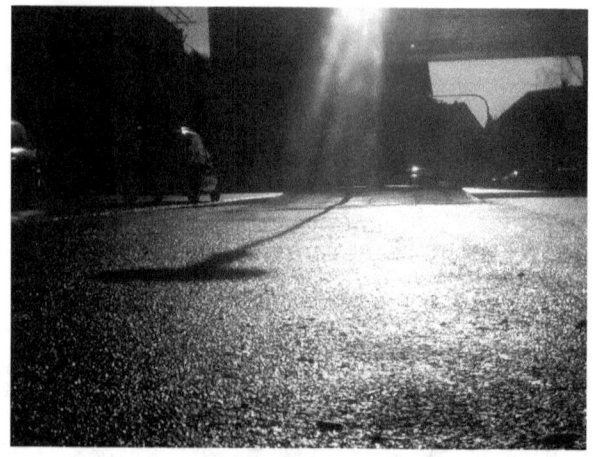

Simone Kaplan   Special Edition :Black & White

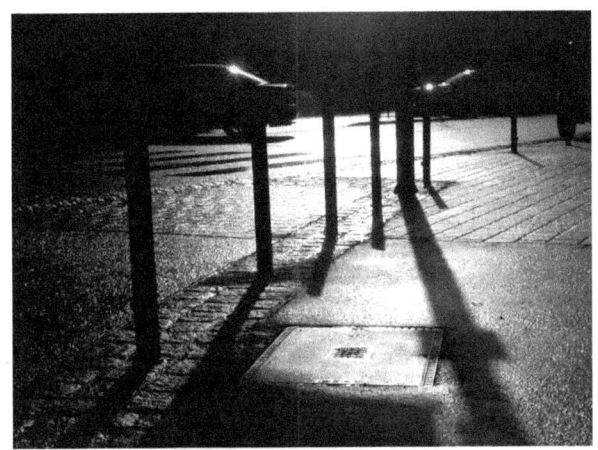

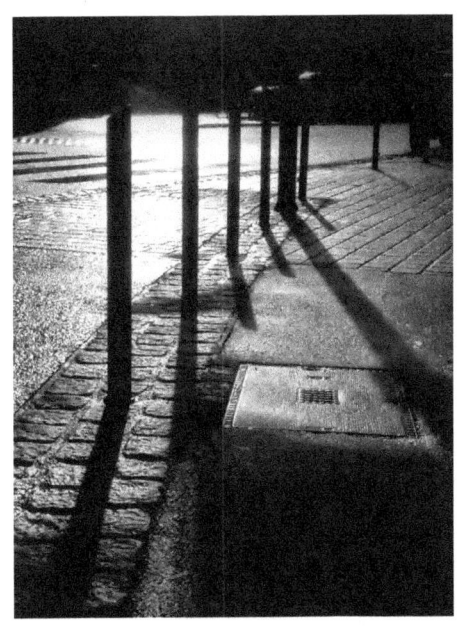

Simone Kaplan Special Edition :Black & White

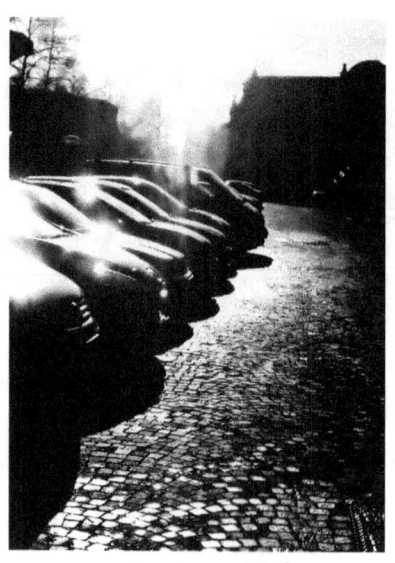

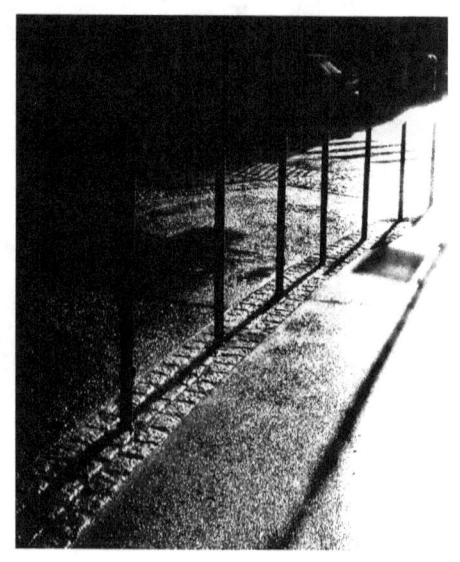

Building Site

Building sites fascinate me as a photographer particularly. It lies in these abstract forms as well as these countless lines, shades and lights. I was so happy, when I could find, finally, a building site. The weather was wonderful and sunny.... but..I was not alone long.
Just I was during foto journey, as two construction workers appeared . When they me to discovered ones they came slowly near and the air was full of dangerous....

In a hurry I snappet my dearly loved camera. Since a camera woke fast suspicion and disagreeable questions. Strangers were not seen on a building site with pleasure. And I thought, would have on peacefull Sunday on the building site. You must be joking...:)
I disappeared in the inside of the building site... the problem was only that I did not find immediately in the saving free field.. I got lost in the tangle of rooms, rubble and concrete bags . But I ran into the saved free field like a scared rabbit...:)
My only thought was the pictures are in the box. Here the result:

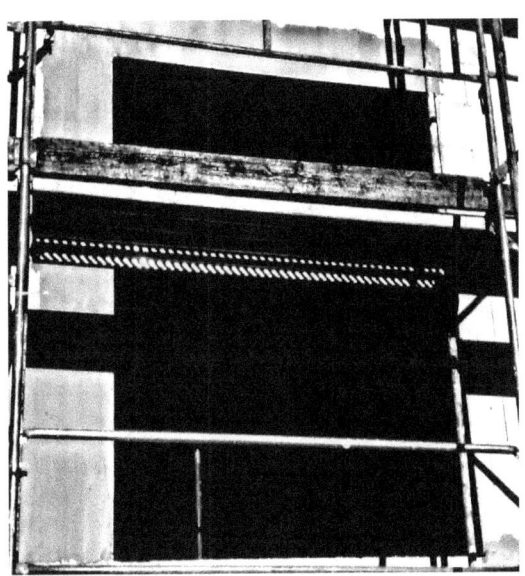

Simone Kaplan Special Edition :Black & White

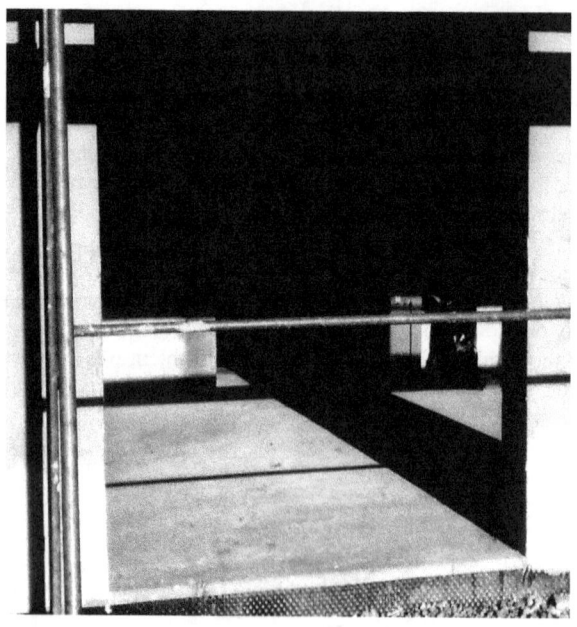

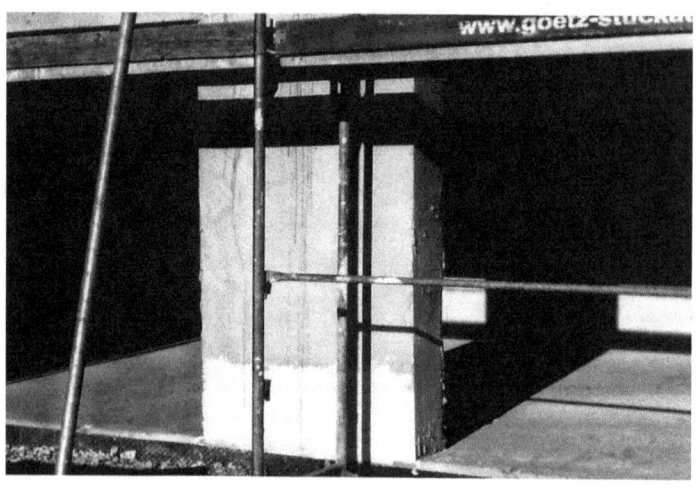

Simone Kaplan Special Edition :Black & White

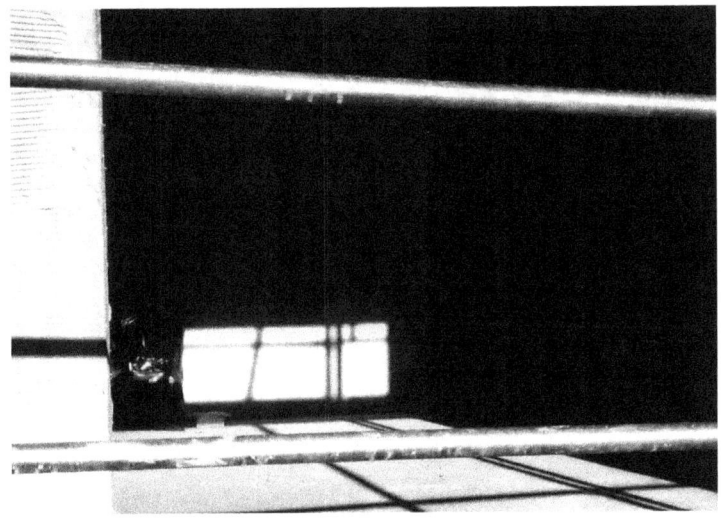

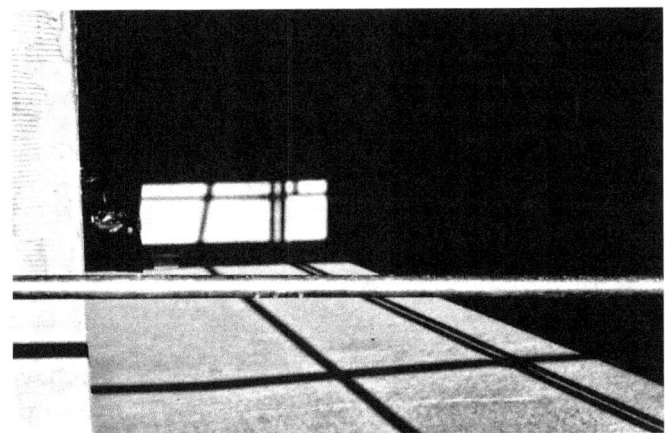

Simone Kaplan				Special Edition :Black & White

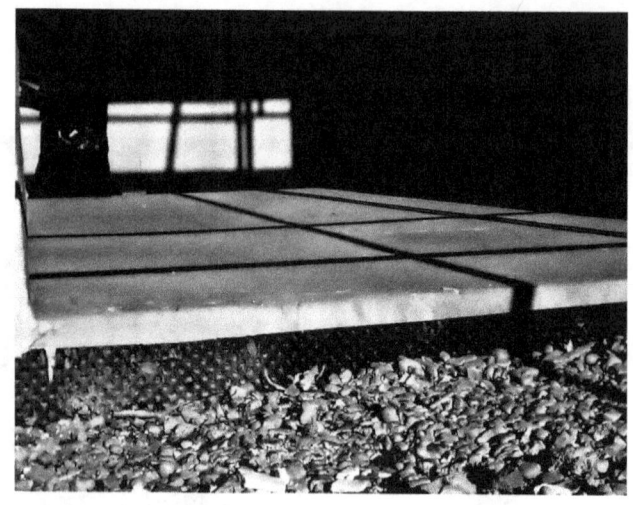

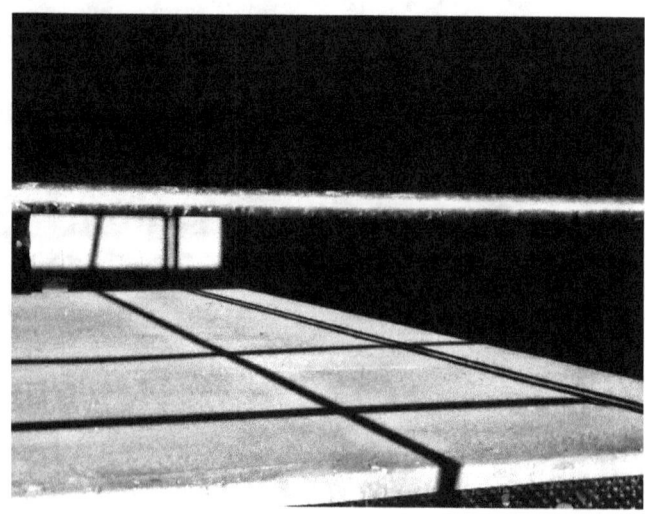

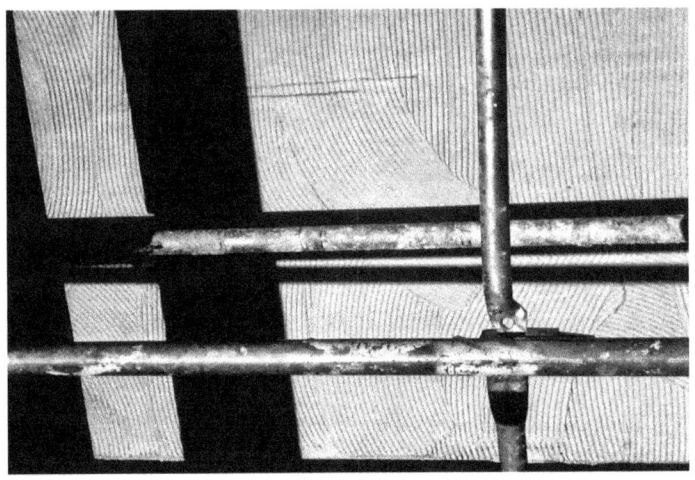

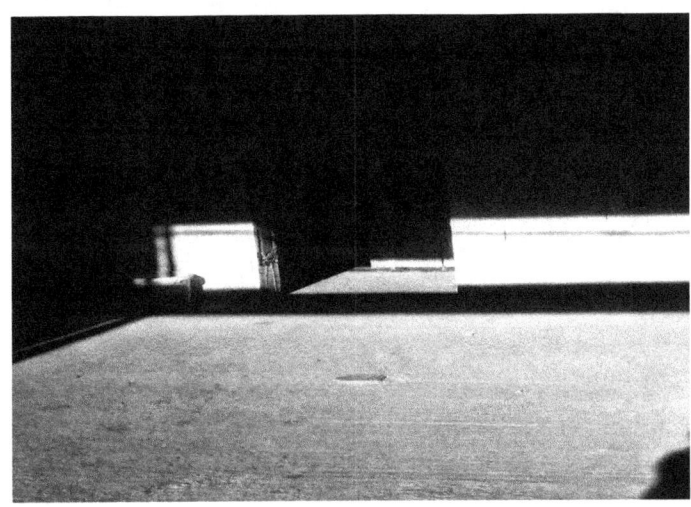

Simone Kaplan Special Edition :Black & White

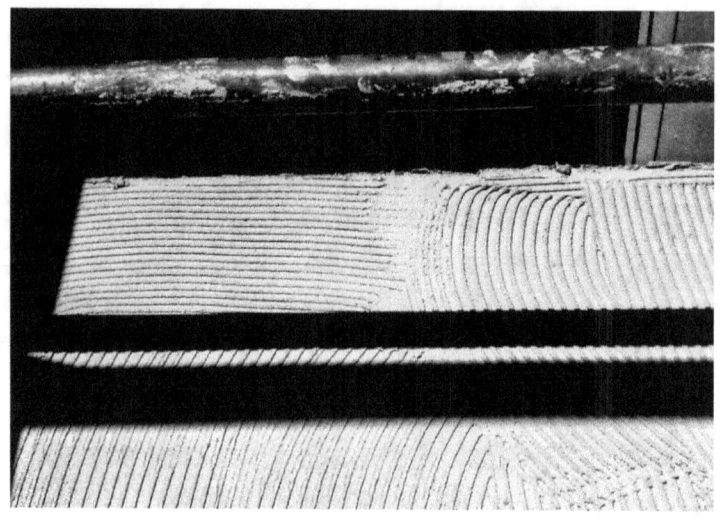

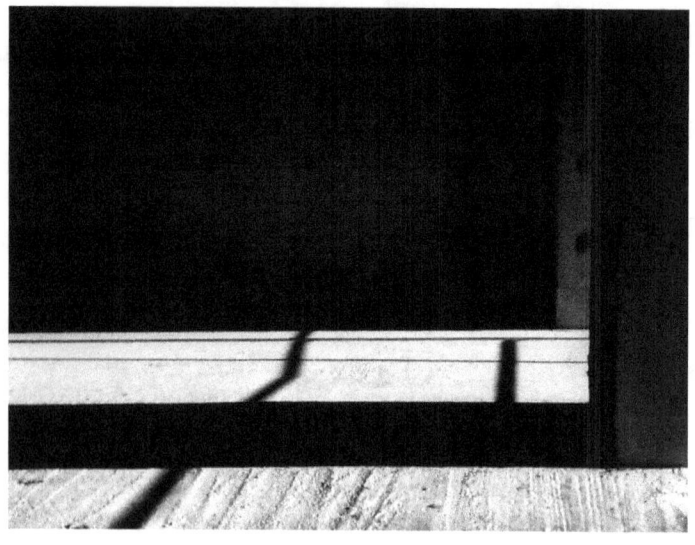

Simone Kaplan · Special Edition :Black & White

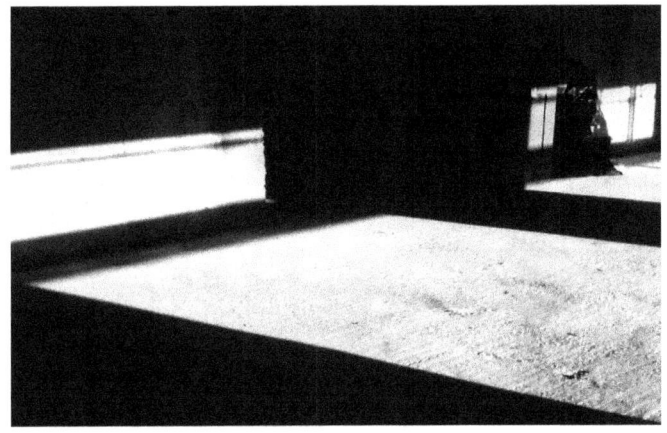

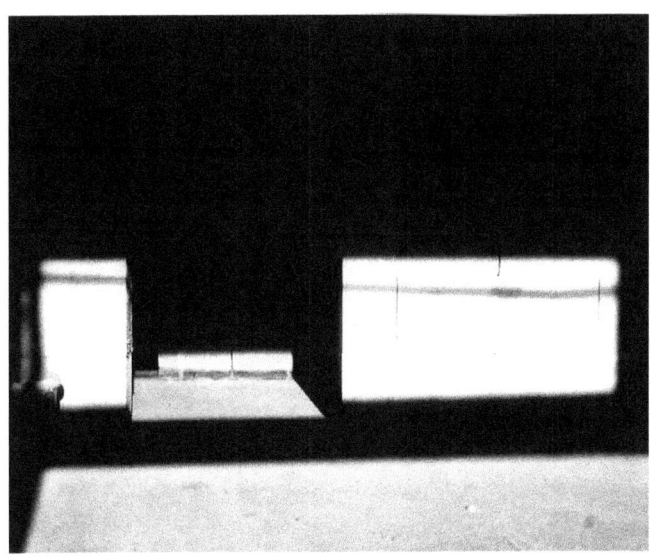

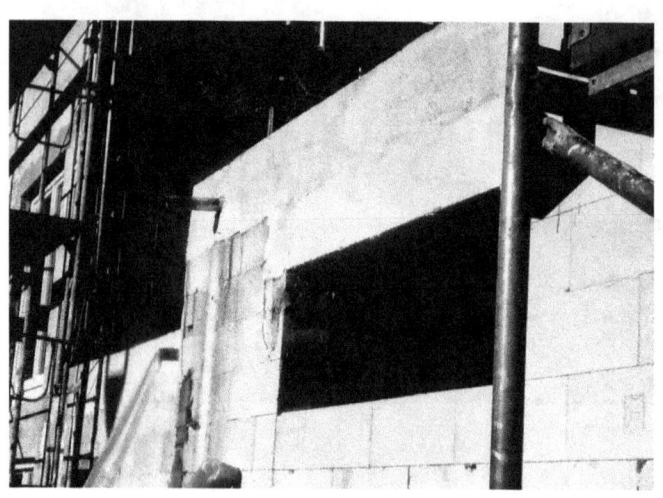

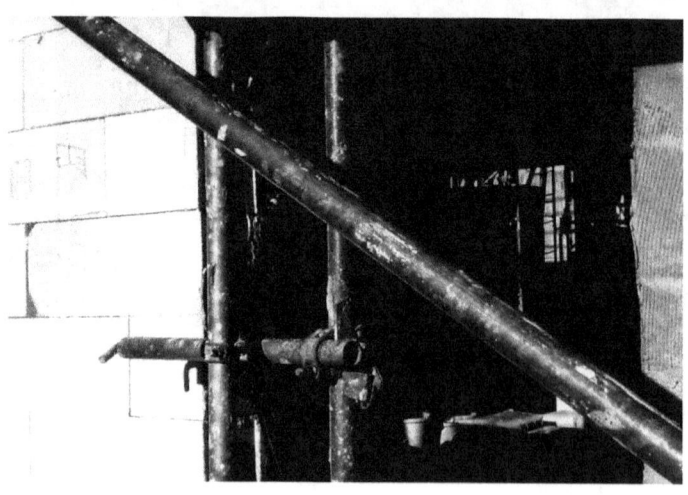

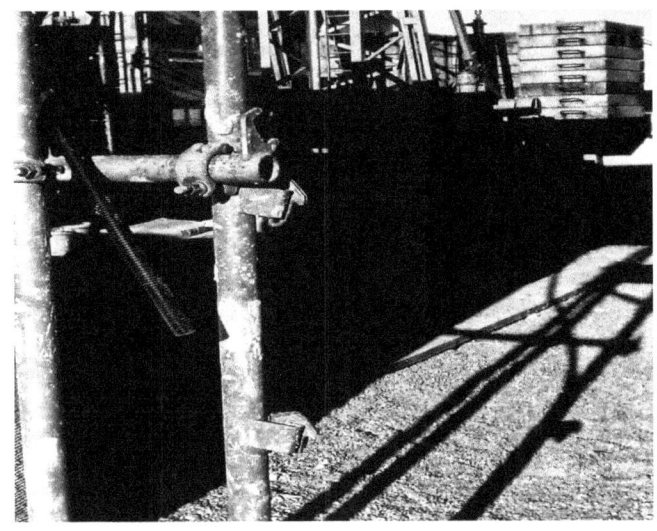

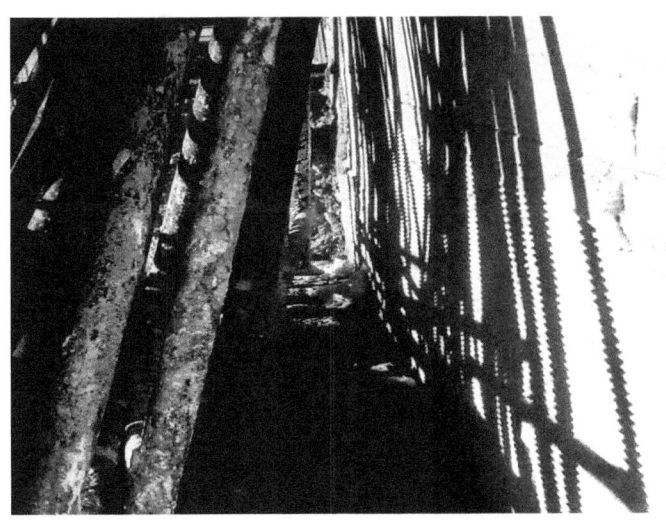

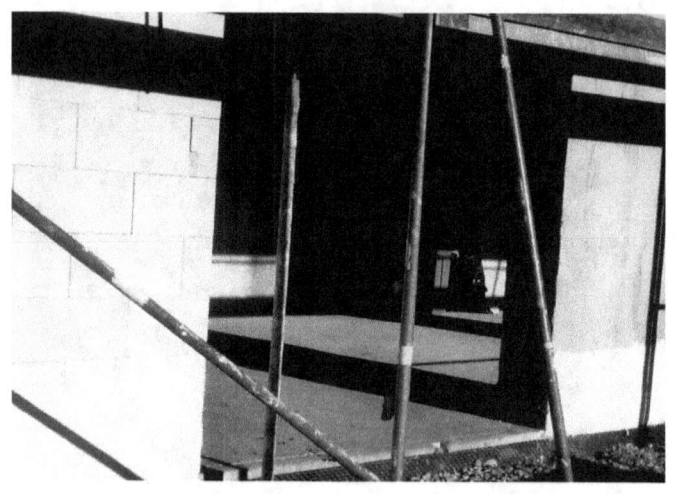

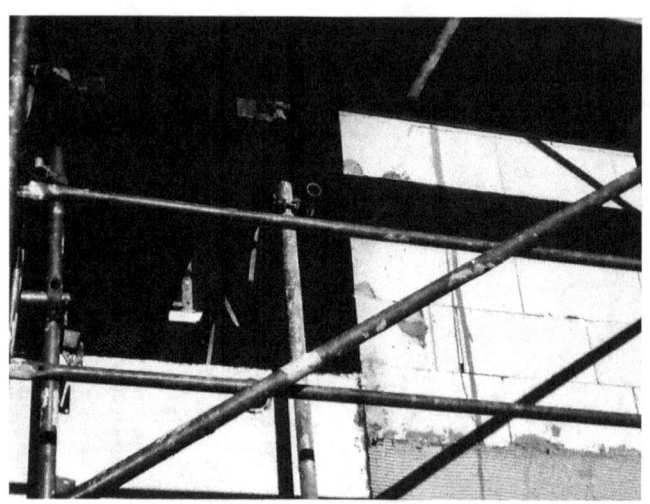

Simone Kaplan   Special Edition :Black & White

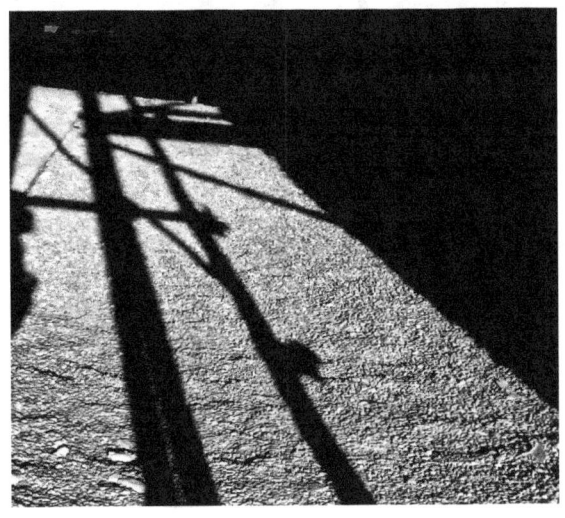

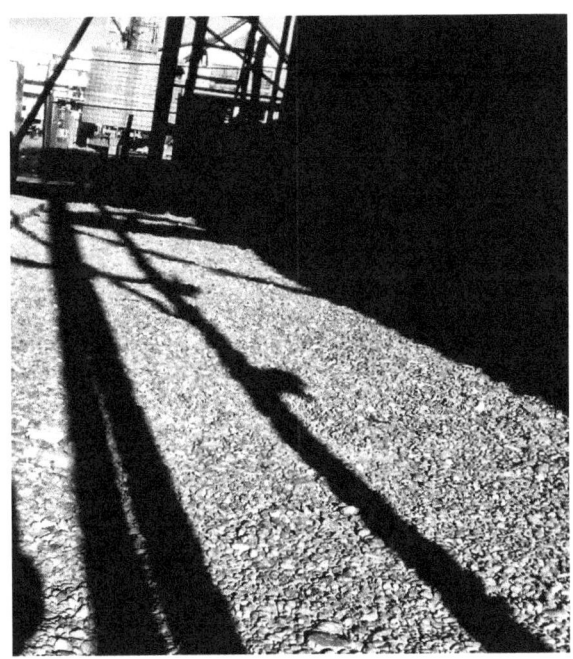

Simone Kaplan   Special Edition :Black & White

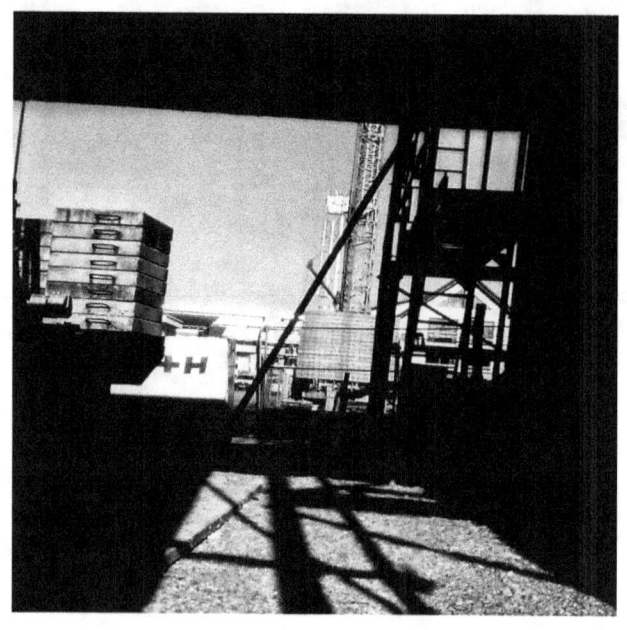

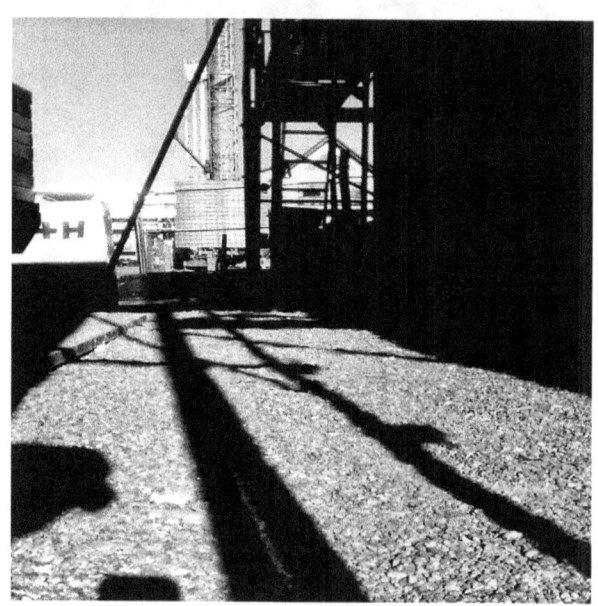

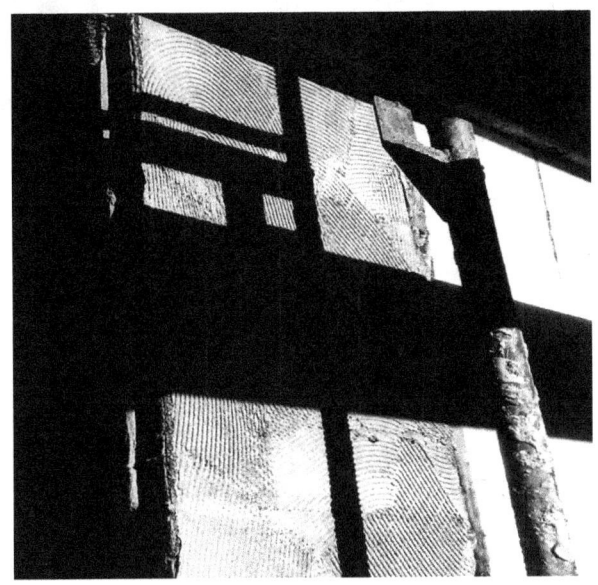

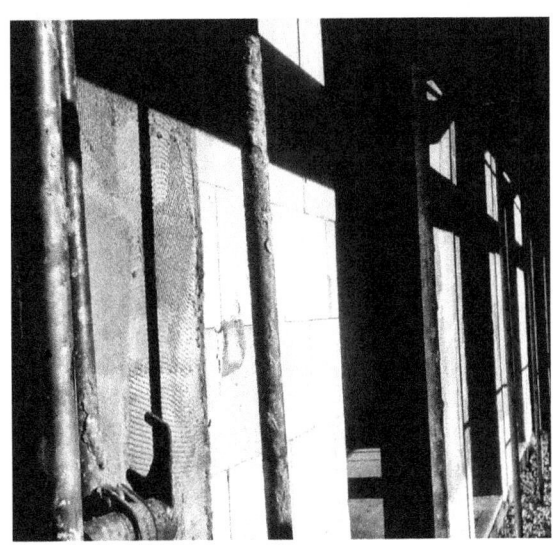

Simone Kaplan　　　　　　　　　　　　　　　　　Special Edition :Black & White

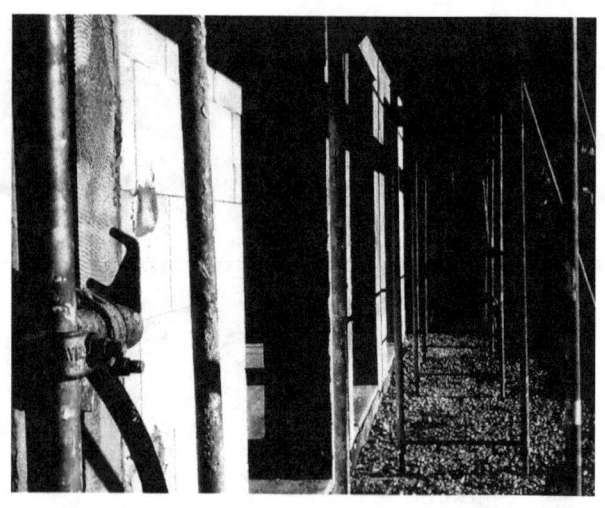

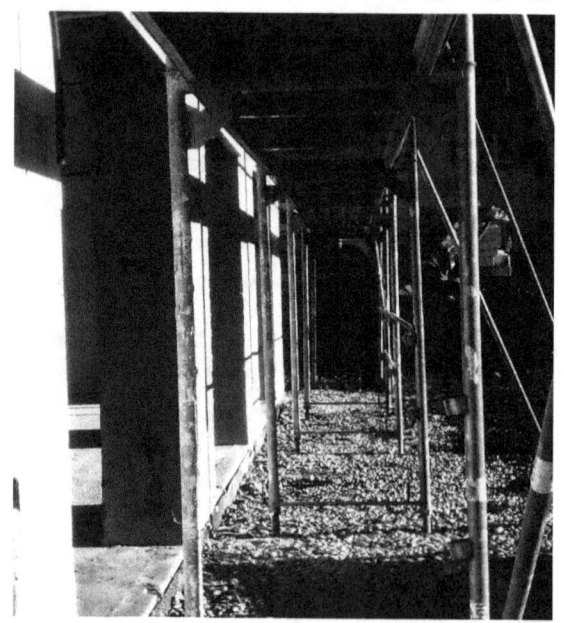

Simone Kaplan   Special Edition :Black & White

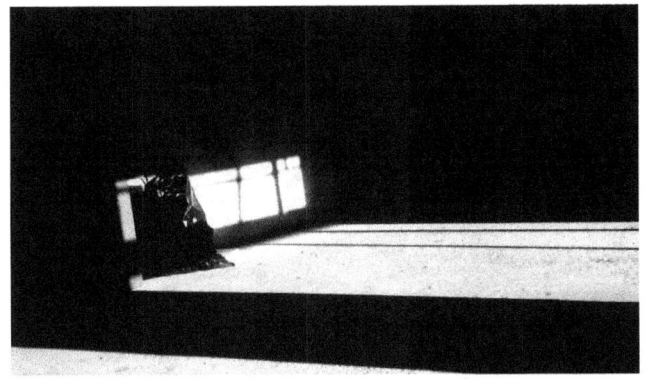

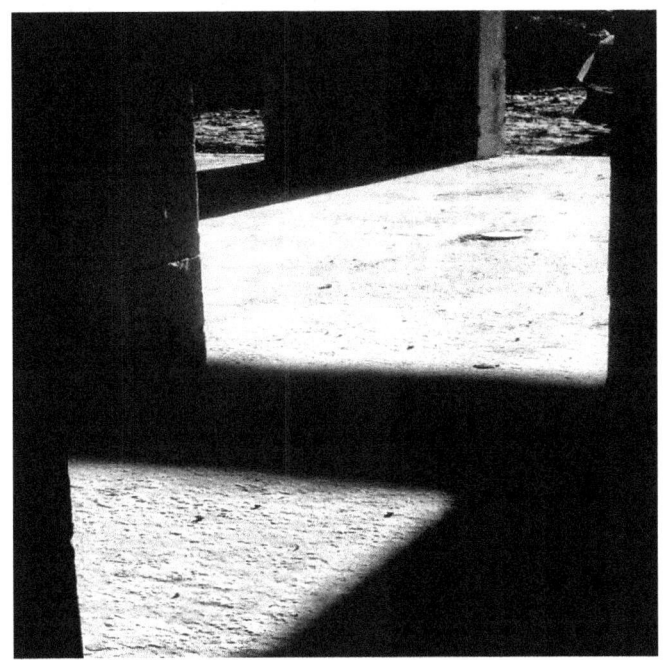

Simone Kaplan　　　　　　　　　　　　　　　　　　　Special Edition :Black & White

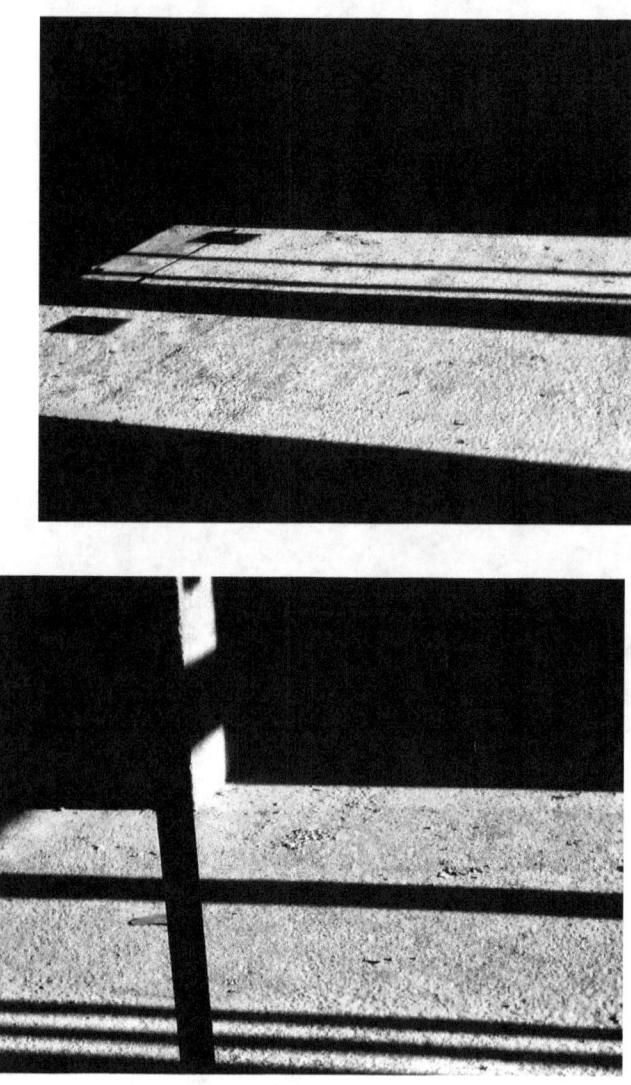

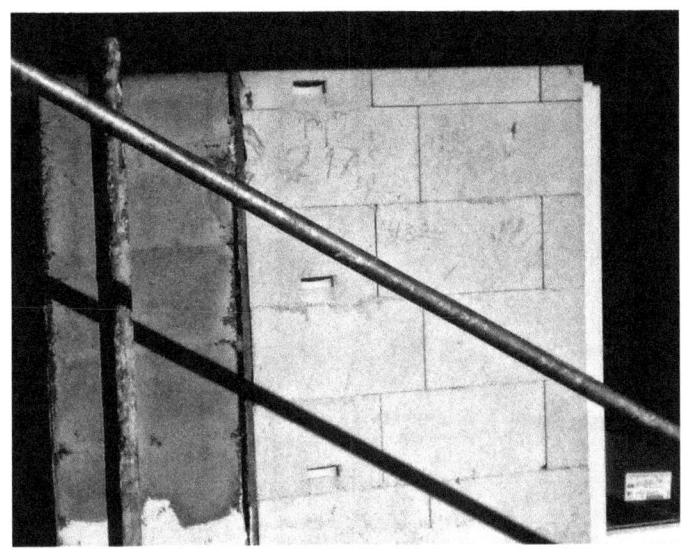

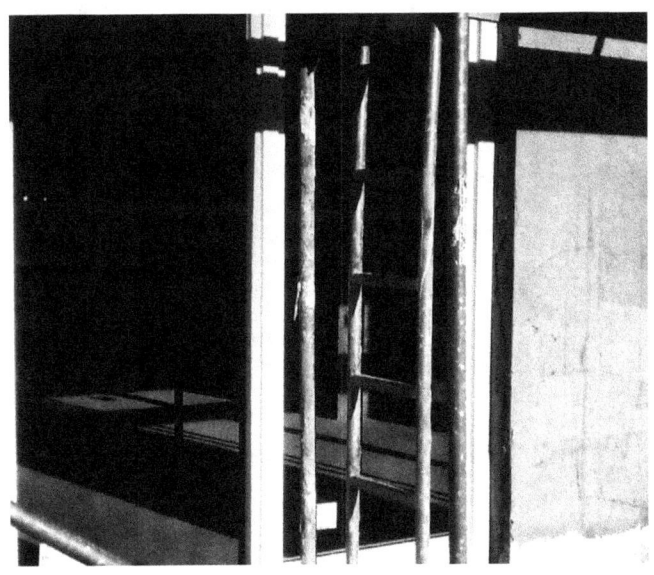

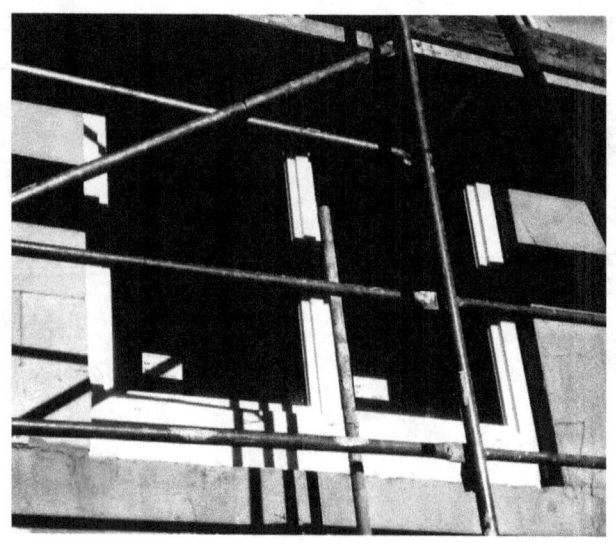

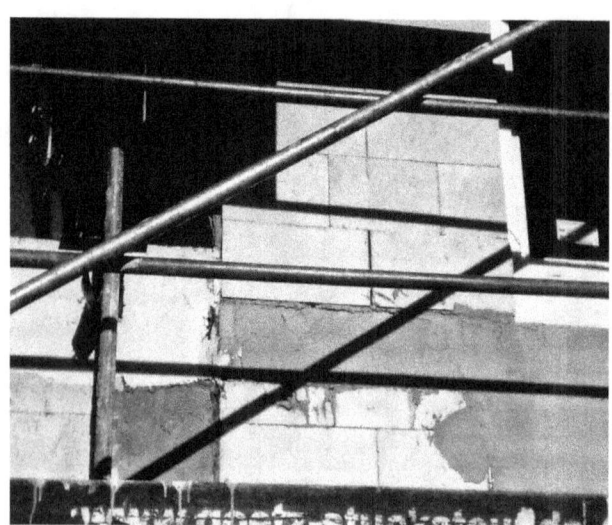

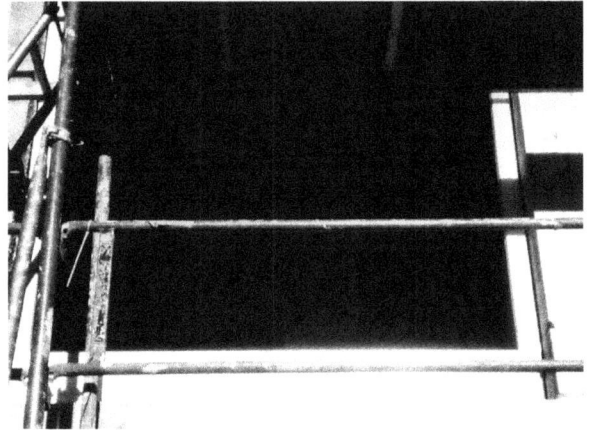

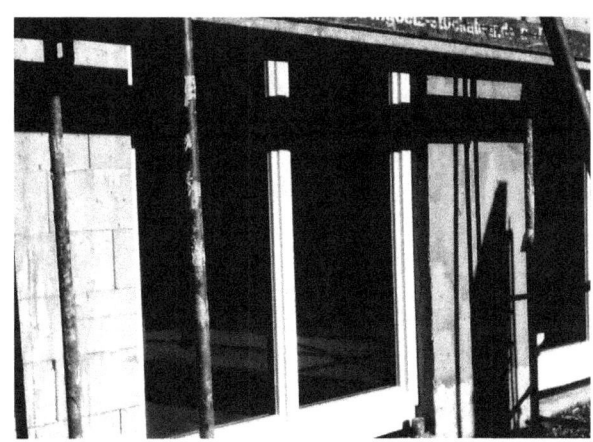

Storm

In the news they announced a storm. This was for me of course a highlight. I love thunderstorm and storm so much.
So I waited tensely for the so largely announced storm. I walked in the wood and looked for sign of a storm.
However, far and wide was blue sky and beaming sunshine. Disappointed I left the wood .

Two days later....
In relaxed mood I walked by the wood .Of course my camera was present and I concentrated upon light and shade . Suddenly I noted a hard gust of wind which roared by the trees...

Curiously and surprised I went to the free area and ..... thick heavy storm clouds were brewing in the horizon together. Now and then the sun still peeped between the heavy cloud benches out and fought laboriously for more place.
And I.... I could press only the trigger... to experience these forces of nature with overpowering joy . Indeed, I forgot that the storm could go off any minute....
Now he went off... and I ran about fields and fields as if it was about my life.
I came along, finally, healthy at home with my camera. :)
Indeed, then I had the next days for the time being enough of slushy, wet fields and morass.:)

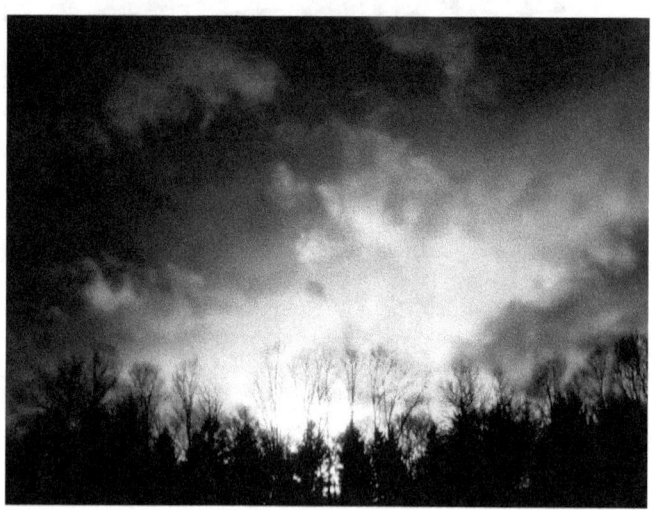

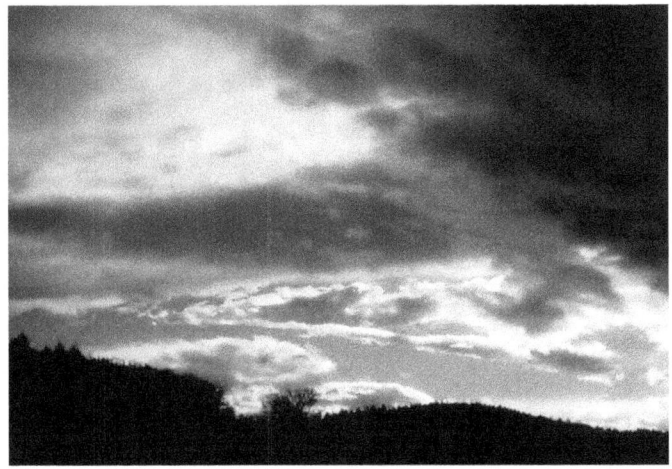

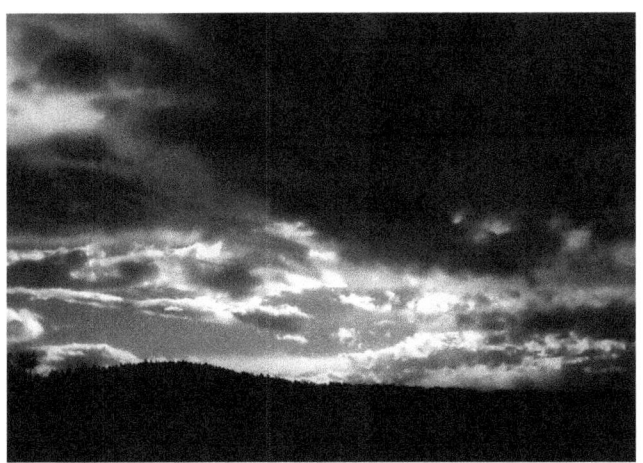

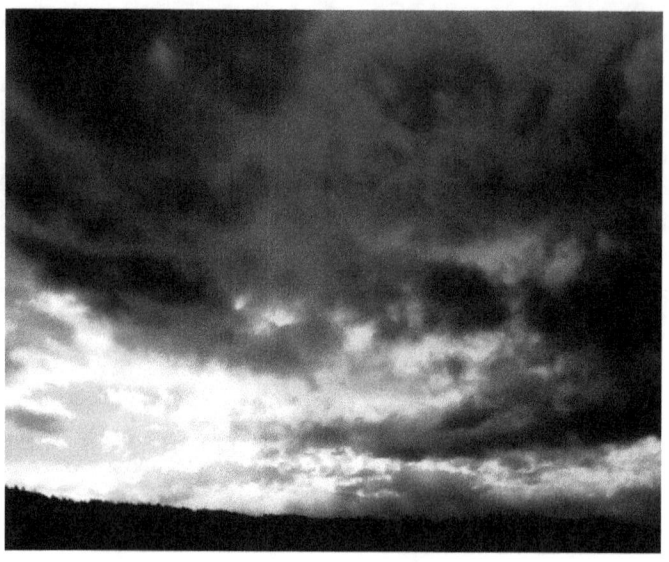

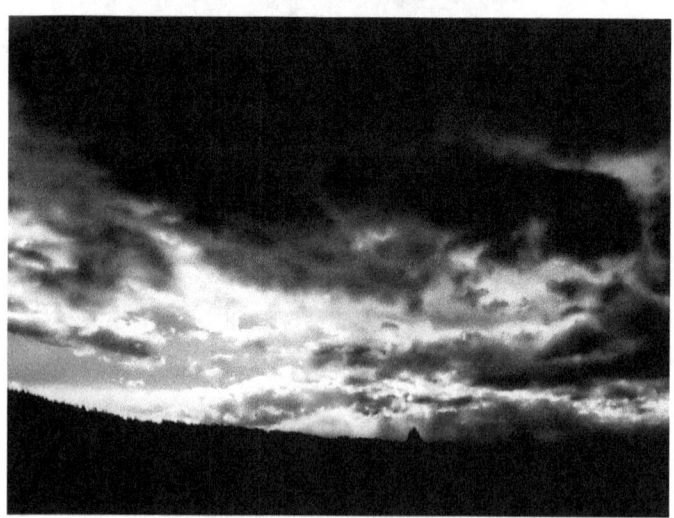

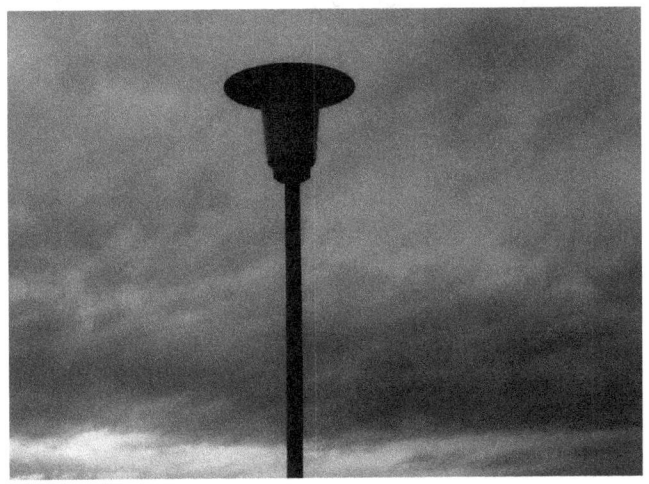

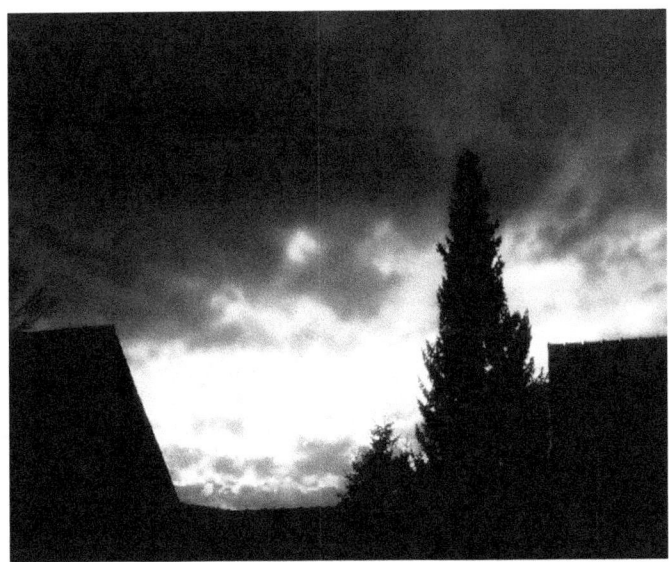

Simone Kaplan Special Edition :Black & White

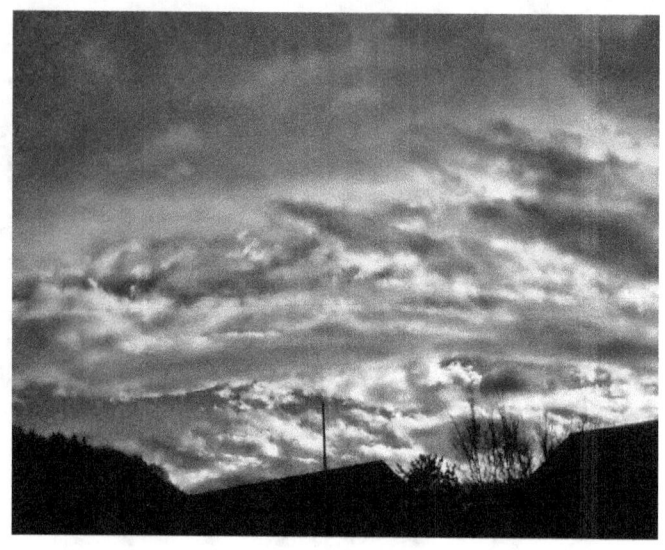

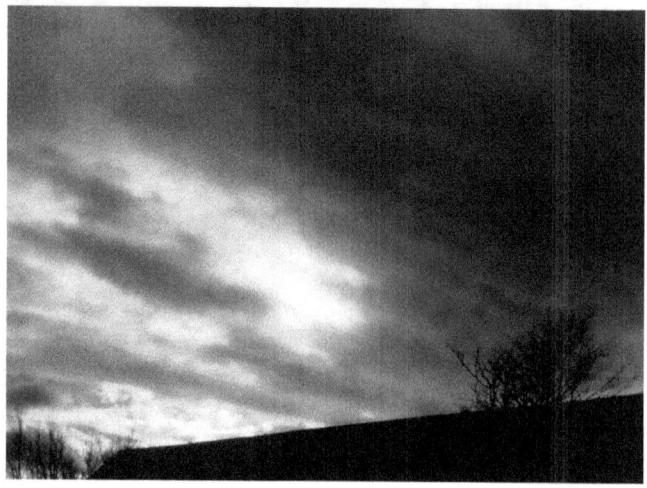

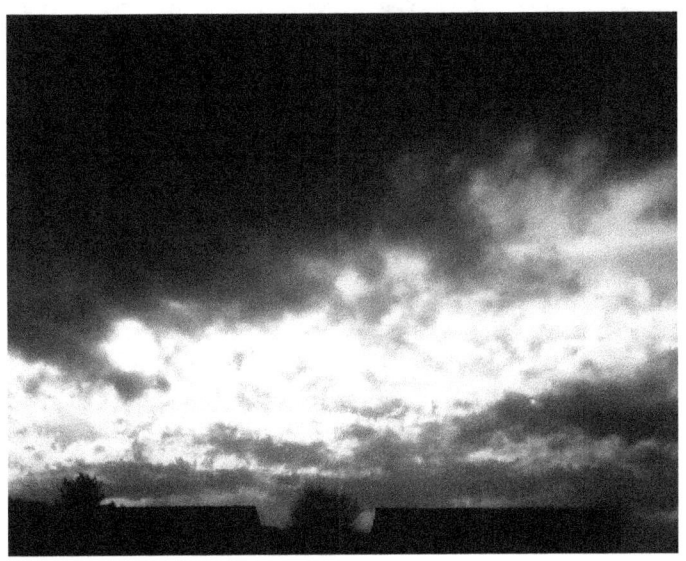

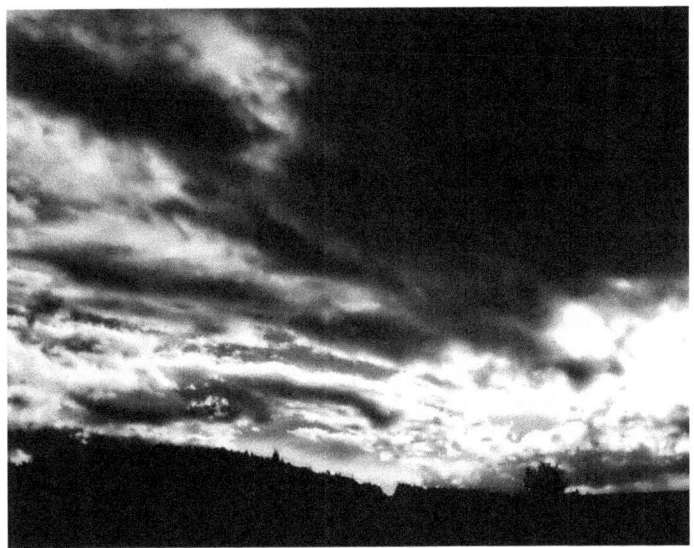

Simone Kaplan   Special Edition :Black & White

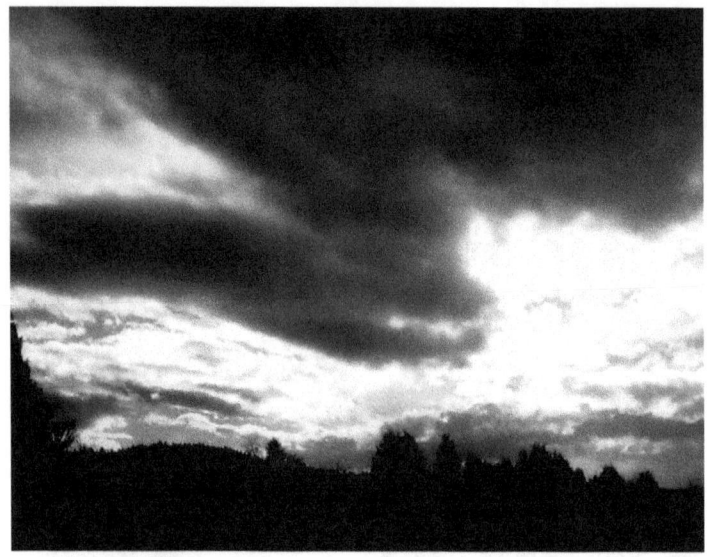

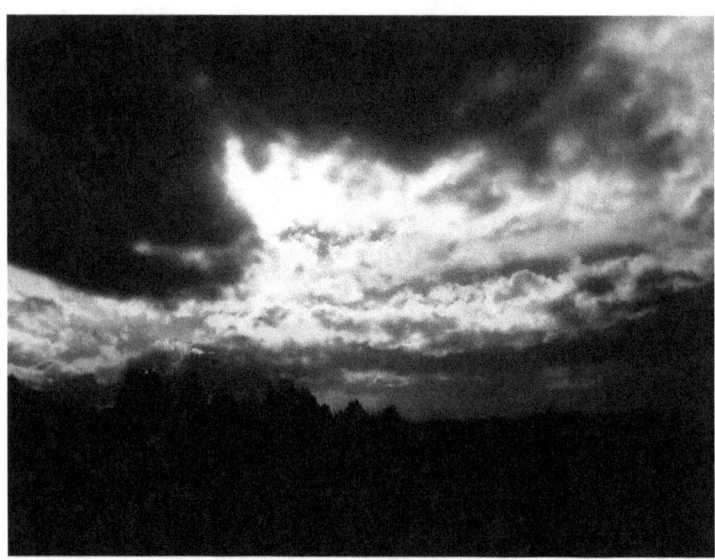

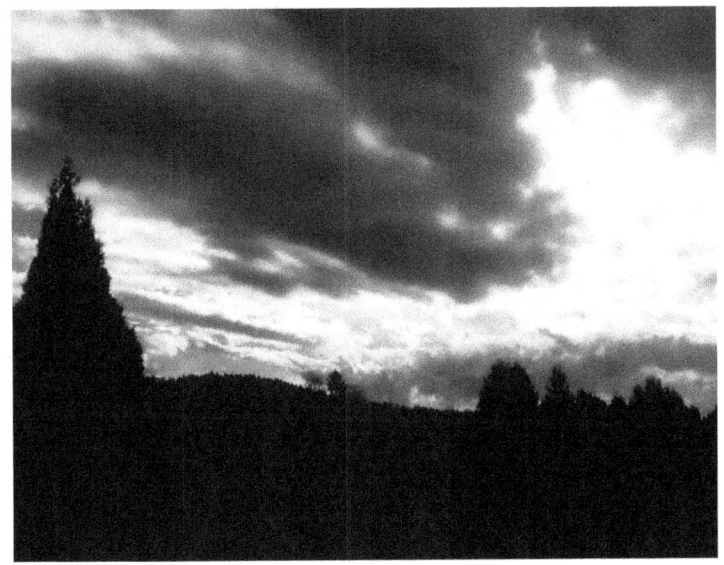

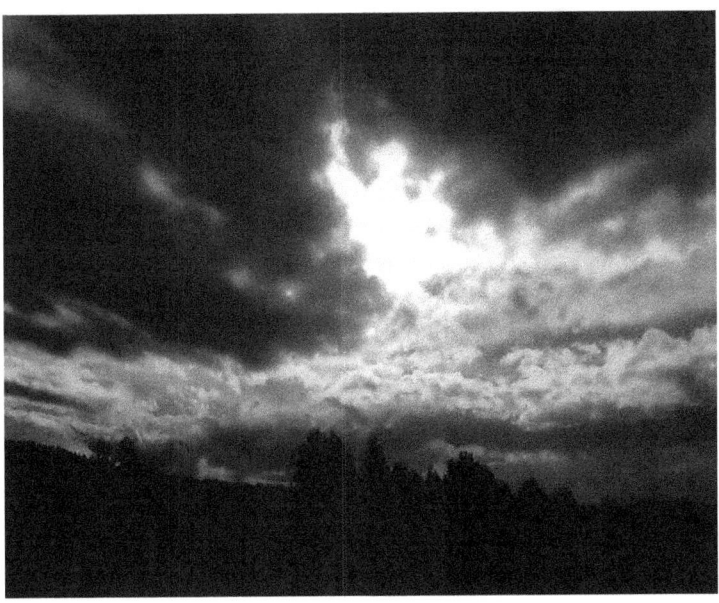

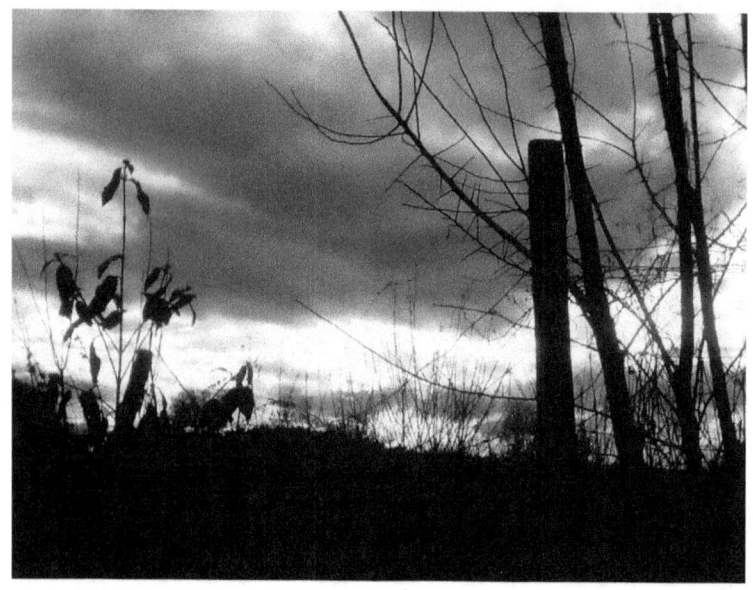

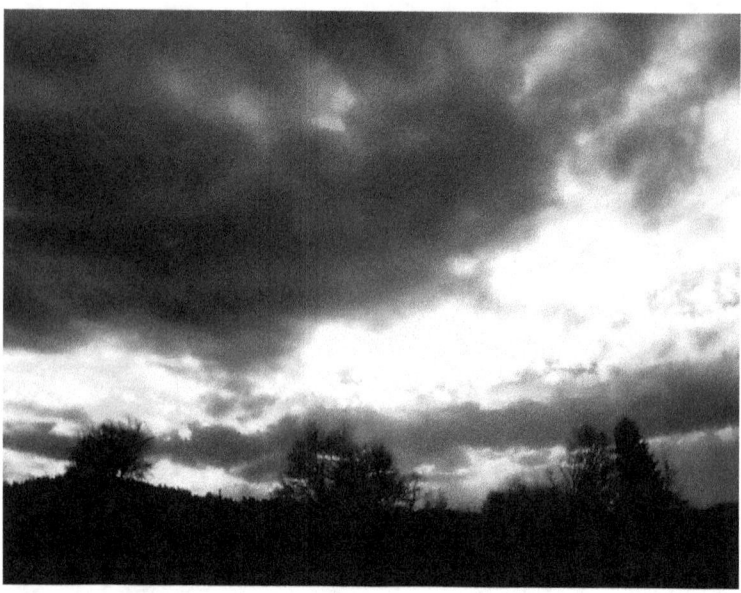

Briefly before the storm broke out, I discovered this small group of the sheep who stood close in a corner.

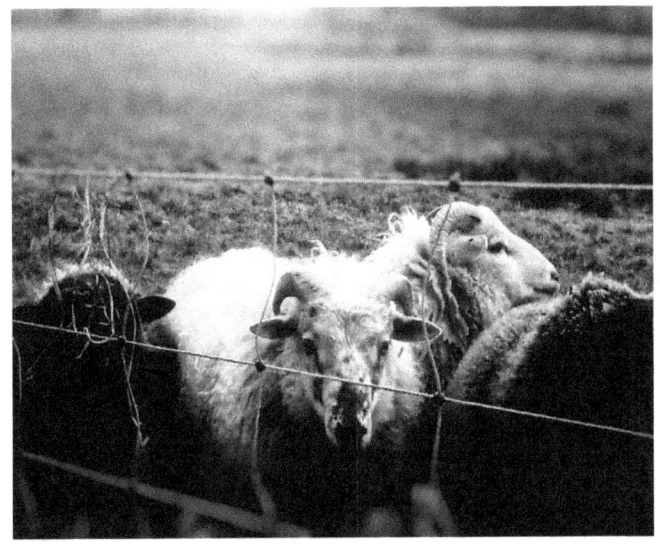

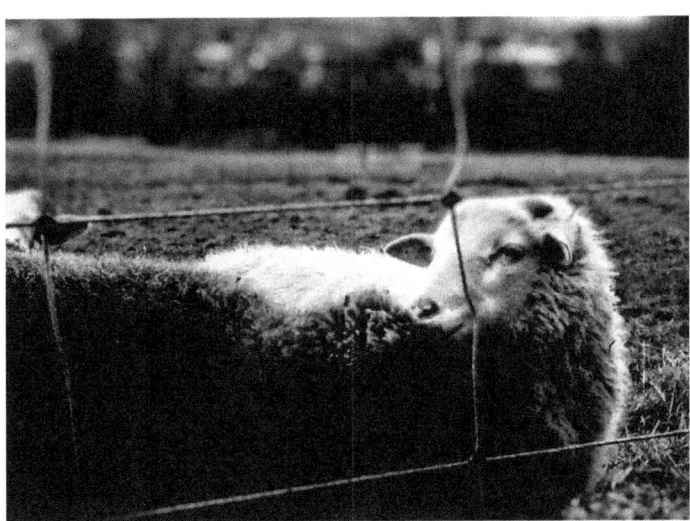

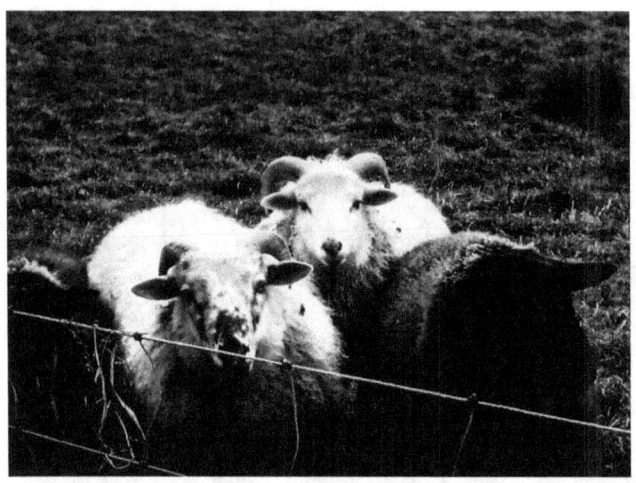

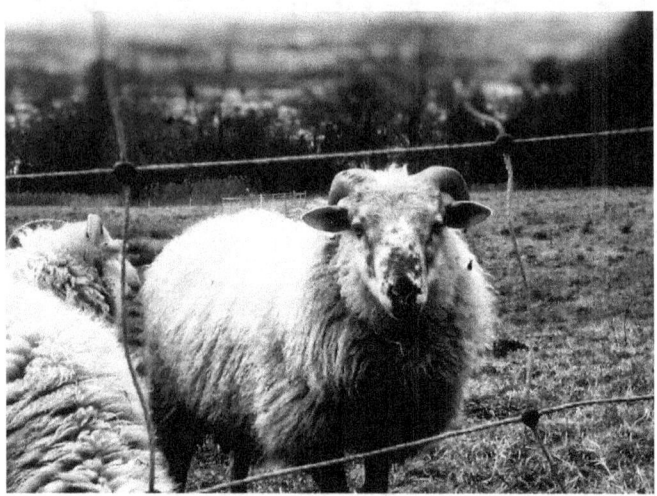

This young ram still wished me best of luck before the storm broke out...:)

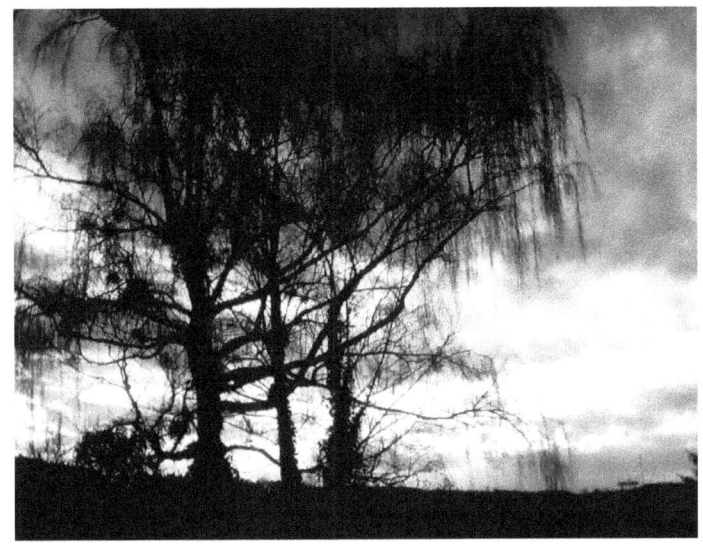

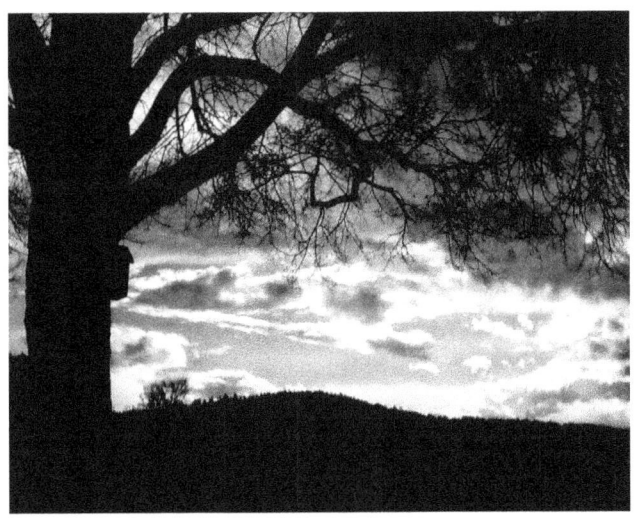

T.H.E   E.N.D

www.ingramcontent.com/pod-product-compliance
Lightning Source LLC
Chambersburg PA
CBHW071826170526
45167CB00003B/1433